GRAMMAR TODAY

Comprising a few more

RULES RUGE

would have espoused

for proper English usage

Compiled by Daniel Hoyt Daniels,
St. Albans School,   Class of 1945

Tradepaper Edition 10-digit ISBN: 1-58218-872-6
Tradepaper Edition 13 digit ISBN: 978-1-58218-8720

First DSI Printing: March 2015

Published by Digital Scanning, Inc. Scituate, MA 02066
781-545-2100
http://www.Digitalscanning.com

RULES RUGE

iii

A Fond Reminiscence
of
Ferdinand E. Ruge

Ferdinand Ruge was an absolutely outstanding teacher, one I remember fondly. He certainly taught me how to write a clear, concise English sentence, and I often wince at some of the poor use of language I read and hear in the media every day. I have to restrain myself occasionally from correcting friends' grammar since it is not considered polite to do so.

I believe the original Ruge Rules and this supplement should be required on the desk of every editor and copywriter in the country. Perhaps some of the corruption could be slowed, and youngsters might learn that "like" is not necessary as a delay word in daily usage. Mr. Ruge would be horrified if he were still with us.

My congratulations and thanks to the author of the present volume for his effort.

Frederic C. Towers, '51

Preface

In the Preface to the Second Edition of "Ruge Rules," published in 1989, Headmaster Paul Piazza invited the submission of new corrections. I have taken the liberty of viewing that invitation loosely and have collected a number of additional points that I think Mr. Ruge would have embraced. I would welcome any comments or corrections to these "additions." I can be contacted through either of the addresses given on page vii.

For the most part, I have limited this endeavor to common errors that I feel are not adequately covered or stressed in many grammar books, and to questionable new expressions and usages. I have tried to ensure that the errors cited herein are clear and that the explanations given are correct.

Certain points made here may suggest other grammatical points that are not covered. Except in rare instances, this book does not address points covered in the book of *Ruge Rules,* which the present reader would do well to obtain or consult, and copies of which I understand can be purchased through the St. Albans School Bookstore, 3001 Wisconsin Avenue, NW Washington, DC 20016. Tel: 202-537-6422

This book is dedicated to the memory of Ferdinand E. Ruge.

Daniel Hoyt Daniels

Foreword

Before I entered St. Albans, I don't think I was ever bothered very much by people's grammatical mistakes. After St. Albans and Ruge, I have lived bearing an awareness of the grammatical errors of people around me -- in college, on the job, in the street, on radio and television, and in newspapers, books, and magazines -- everywhere. I would now like to unload myself of this burden and pass it along, letting others carry it who are younger and more vigorous than I am.

If any readers of this little book should have different or conflicting views regarding any of the items herein, so much the better if they provoke discussion or debate.. I should be interested in learning of any such divergent views and can be reached through addresses given on page vii. I believe it is important for people to think about the words they use and how they put them together.

Daniel Hoyt Daniels

Note to the Reader

This book is neither authorized, funded, approved, nor endorsed by St. Albans School. The author, Daniel Hoyt Daniels, a St. Albans graduate, Class of 1945, is the only one responsible and to blame. Ferdinand E. Ruge was his English teacher in the Fourth, Fifth, and Sixth Forms. It is to the memory of Mr. Ruge that this book is dedicated.

Most of these examples of incorrect or questionable grammar and word usage have been taken from quotes by famous people in important places. These include St. Albans graduates, Harvard graduates, Presidents of the United States, Cabinet Members and Congressmen, Corporate CEO'S, Ph.D. university professors, members of Mensa and the Triple Nine Society, as well as Nobel- and Pulitzer-Prize-winning authors, who should know better. Let's stamp out bad English.

Sources of most of the errors and quotations cited herein are available from the author upon request.

Daniel Hoyt Daniels   or   Daniel Hoyt Daniels
PMB 47, Suite B   PO Box 1681
2724 61st Street   Beaufort, SC 29901
Galveston, TX 77551   843-846-0123

April 2015   danielhdaniels@yahoo.com

CONTENTS

Abbreviations -- Use of

It is preferable, in formal prose, to limit the use of abbreviations such as "US" to cases in which they serve as adjectives.

Inferior: I am one of those who believe that it would be a mistake for the US to take unilateral action.

Better: I am one of those who believe that it would be a mistake for the United States to take unilateral action.

Acceptable: I would oppose US intervention.

Acceptable: US ground troops have entered the country.

Poor: StA is a fine school.

Better: St. Albans is a fine school.

or: Saint Albans is a fine school.

Acceptable: The StA football team has an outstanding record.

Adjective Used as Adverb -- Exact Same, Likely

Adjectives modify nouns; adverbs modify verbs, adjectives, or other adverbs. A few adjectives, including likely, heavenly, stately, *and* ugly, *end in -ly and may give the misleading appearance of being adverbs.*

Incorrect: The Gospel of John says the exact same thing.

Incorrect: The Gospel of John says the same exact thing.

Correct: The Gospel of John says exactly the same thing.

"Exact" and "same" are both adjectives; one cannot modify the other.

Incorrect: It will likely rain.

Correct: It is likely to rain.

Correct: Rain is likely.

Likely is an adjective, although it has the appearance of an adverb because it ends in -ly. The misuse of likely *has become so prevalent that* likely *is beginning to appear in cheap modern dictionaries as an adverb.*

Incorrect: I love King Arthur Bread Flour; it bakes heavenly.

It is easy to misuse adjectives as adverbs when they end in -ly, as do "likely" and "heavenly." Of course, most words ending in -ly are indeed adverbs. Maybe there is the potential for a new word here, heavenly-ly, *which is what was meant.*

Incorrect: Mr. Ruge is a real good teacher.

Correct: Mr. Ruge is a really good teacher.
  (Really is an adverb modifying *good.)*

Correct: Mr. Ruge really is a good teacher.
  (Really is an adverb modifying *is.)*

Agreement of Subject and Verb

Use care to ensure that the subject and verb agree in number.

Incorrect: This secret list of articles and rules were signed by each member of the crew.

Correct: This secret list of articles and rules *was* signed by each member of the crew.

Incorrect: Blackbeard was a tall man, at a time when the average person was shorter than they are now.

Correct: Blackbeard was a tall man, at a time when the average person was shorter than *he is* now.

Correct: Blackbeard was a tall man, at a time when average *people* were shorter than they are now.

Incorrect: Amanda Knox, together with her boyfriend, were arrested and are being held in custody.

Correct: Amanda Knox, together with her boyfriend, *was* arrested and *is* being held in custody.

Correct: Amanda Knox *and* her boyfriend were arrested and are being held in custody.

Incorrect: Each of you are heirs of peacemakers who imagined the world as it should be.

Correct: Each of you *is an heir* of peacemakers who imagined the world as it should be.

Correct: *All of you* are heirs of peacemakers who imagined the world as it should be.

Incorrect: The validity of these programs are being challenged.

Correct: The validity of these programs *is* being challenged.

Alright -- All Right

All right *is correct.* Alright *does not exist in the older Webster unabridged dictionaries. Unfortunately, it is beginning to appear in some of the cheap newer editions.*

Substandard: He owed Jessica a hundred dollars, but that was alright because Jessica also took markers.

Correct: He owed Jessica a hundred dollars, but that was all right because Jessica also took markers.

Appraise -- Apprise

Appraise *and* apprise *are often confused.* Appraise *means* to evaluate. Apprise *means* to inform.

Incorrect: Before we bombed Tripoli we appraised the Soviet Union.

Correct: Before we bombed Tripoli we apprised the Soviet Union (of our intentions).

Correct: The insurance agent appraised my car at $1,850.

Correct: He then apprised the company of his findings.

Collective Nouns

Collective nouns, such as family, group, couple, team, *may be considered singular or plural, as is called for by the context or intention of the writer. However, consistency is required: a collective noun cannot be both singular and plural in the same sentence or expression.*

Incorrect: Another group of former NHL players has joined the fight for compensation for head injuries they say they incurred while playing.

Correct: Another group of former NHL players *have* joined the fight for compensation for head injuries they say they incurred while playing.

Grammatically correct, but illogical: Another group of former NHL players has joined the fight for compensation for head injuries it says it incurred while playing.

Incorrect: Arnold Schwarzenegger indicated in a court filing that he does not want to pay wife Maria Shriver spousal support or attorney fees as the couple ends their 25-year marriage.

Correct: Arnold Schwarzenegger indicated in a court filing that he does not want to pay wife Maria Shriver spousal support or attorney fees as the couple *end* their 25-year marriage.

Grammatically correct: Arnold Schwarzenegger indicated in a court filing that he does not want to pay wife Maria Shriver spousal support or attorney fees as the couple *ends its* 25-year marriage.

Incorrect: An entire generation of Cubans has been told their suffering has been caused by the American embargo.

Correct: An entire generation of Cubans *have* been told their suffering has been caused by the American embargo..

Also correct: An entire generation of Cubans has been told *its* suffering has been caused by the American embargo.

Commas on Parenthetical Expressions

If a parenthetical expression within a sentence is to be set off by commas, two commas are required.

Incorrect: I told Malia once that during the entire time that I was growing up, I attended exactly two birthday parties.

Correct: I told Malia once that, during the entire time that I was growing up, I attended exactly two birthday parties.

If the expression "during the entire time that I was growing up" is to be set off by commas, two commas are required: fore and aft. One comma does not suffice.

Incorrect: Hamilton and several others found it mind-boggling that given the critical problems, Rumsfeld would single out these sideline issues.

Correct: Hamilton and several others found it mind-boggling that, given the critical problems, Rumsfeld would single out these sideline issues.

If there is to be a comma after problems, *there must be one before* given.

Incorrect: Evidence shows that by changing the default rule, employee participation rates go up dramatically.

Better: Evidence shows that, by changing the default rule, employee participation rates go up dramatically.

If there is to be a comma after rule, *there must be one before* by.

Better still: Evidence shows that, *when the default rule is changed,* employee participation rates go up dramatically. (*to avoid the dangling gerund*)

Comparison of Adjectives

Some adjectives do not properly admit of comparison. Examples include inevitable, square, circular, unique, complete, ideal, exact, and perfect. *However, common usage often allows us to neglect application of this rather antiquated rule.*

Traditionally incorrect: Use the piece that is the squarest.

Correct: Use the piece that is most nearly square.

Traditionally incorrect: This is the most complete collection ever assembled.

Correct: This is the most nearly complete collection ever assembled.

Incorrect: ... in order to form a more perfect union ...

Correct: ... in order to form a more nearly perfect union ...

Incorrect: I have learned, by the perfectest report, they have more in them than knowledge.

Correct: I have learned, by the most nearly perfect report, they have more in them than knowledge.

Correct: I have learned, by the best available report, they have more in them than knowledge.

Comprise – Constitute -- Compose

Do not use "is comprised of" to mean "is composed of."

Comprise means to *encompass* or *include*. It does not mean to *constitute*. It may mean to *consist of*. The whole *comprises* the parts. The parts, taken together, *constitute* the whole.

Incorrect: New England is *comprised of* six states.

Correct: New England *comprises* six states.

Correct: New England is *composed of* six states.

Correct: Six states *constitute* New England..

Correct: The plain but abundant fare *comprised* oysters stewed with saffron, boiled crabs, soles fried in butter, suckling-pig seethed in milk, roast capons, titbits of lamb spitted between slices of onion, a simple, sweet confection of honey and eggs and cream, and a deep Samian pitcher of home-brewed mead.

Correct: The plain but abundant fare *consisted of* oysters stewed with saffron, boiled crabs, soles fried in butter, suckling-pig seethed in milk, roast capons, titbits of lamb spitted between slices of onion, a simple, sweet confection of honey and eggs and cream, and a deep Samian pitcher of home-brewed mead.

Correct: Oysters stewed with saffron, boiled crabs, soles fried in butter, suckling-pig seethed in milk, roast capons, titbits of lamb spitted between slices of onion, a simple, sweet confection of honey and eggs and cream, and a deep Samian pitcher of home-brewed mead -- *constituted* the plain but abundant fare.

Incorrect: Now there was only one ship left of the five comprising the original Armada de Molucca.

Correct: Now there was only one ship left of the five constituting the original Armada de Molucca.

Correct: Now there was only one ship left of the five that the original Armada de Molucca had comprised.

Dangling Participles and Gerunds

A dangling participle or gerund is one without a logical subject, clearly expressed.

Incorrect: After having traveled to Hawaii to visit my grandmother, the state legislature was called into special session.

Who traveled to Hawaii, the legislature? The subject of "having traveled" must be expressed. This sentence also contains a tense sequence error. "After having traveled" should read either "After traveling" or "Having traveled."

Correct: After I traveled to Hawaii to visit my grandmother, the state legislature was called into session.

Correct: After traveling to Hawaii to visit my grandmother, I learned the state legislature was called into session.

Correct: Having traveled to Hawaii to visit my grandmother, I learned the state legislature was called into session.

Incorrect: While rounding the Royal Sovereign Lighthouse, the wind was blowing forty knots.

Correct: While *we* were rounding the Royal Sovereign Lighthouse, the wind was blowing forty knots.

It was not the wind that was rounding the lighthouse; the subject of rounding needs to be expressed.

Correct: While our boat was rounding the Royal Sovereign Lighthouse, the wind was blowing forty knots.

Incorrect: After reviewing the play action, the ruling on the field is confirmed.

Correct: The play action has been reviewed, and the ruling on the field is confirmed.

Definite -- Definitive

Definite *and* definitive *are often confused or misused.*
Definite *means* clear *and* certain.
Definitive *means* authoritative *or* conclusive.

Incorrect: My wife has definitive opinions on almost every subject you can think of.

Correct: My wife has definite opinions on almost every subject you can think of.

Incorrect: He has invited her to go on a cruise with him next month, and he wants a definitive answer.

Correct: He has invited her to go on a cruise with him next month, and he wants a definite answer. (clear and certain)

Correct: In the case of Roe versus Wade the Supreme Court gave a definitive opinion on the matter of abortion rights. (authoritative)

Questionable: The company has finally issued a definite report giving the details of its oil holdings in Iraq.

Correct: The company has finally issued a definitive report giving the details of its oil holdings in Iraq.

Each Other -- One Another

Use each other *when two people (or items) are involved. Use* one another *when more than two are involved.*

Incorrect: Samuel and Jessie were happiest when they were with one another.

Correct: Samuel and Jessie were happiest when they were with *each other.*

Incorrect: The four Johnson brothers were always arguing with each other.

Correct: The four Johnson brothers were always arguing with *one another.*

Between -- Among

The same rule holds for between *and* among. *Use* between *when two are involved; use* among *when more than two are involved.*

Incorrect: He divided his estate equally between all of us -- my sister, my two brothers, and me.

Correct; He divided his estate equally *among* all of us -- my sister, my two brothers, and me.

Incorrect: Henry and his wife had a few arguments among themselves.

Correct: Henry and his wife had a few arguments *between* themselves.

Correct: The four Johnson brothers were always arguing among themselves.

Expectations -- Goals and Objectives

Expectation *means one's* best estimate of what will occur. *Like* prediction, *it is what one* anticipates *or believes is* most likely to happen. *Unfortunately it is often used to mean* goal *or* objective.

Poor: If we want our students to do better, we should raise our expectations.

Correct: If we want our students to do better, we should raise our *goals.*

Correct: My expectation is that I will get at least an 80 on our next English text.

Better: I expect to get at least on 80 on our next English test.

Correct: I expected to get at least an 80 on our last English test, but got only 74.

Better yet: I expected to make at least an 80 on our last English test, but made only 74. (avoiding the "get - got" habit)

Correct: The expectations of the pollsters turned out to be very accurate after the last election.

Incorrect: In the future I will expect you to get straight A's, do you hear?

Correct: In the future I want you to get straight A's.

Correct: In the future I want your goal to be straight A's.

Correct: Some of Charles Dickens' characters never fulfilled their expectations.

False Ellipsis

An ellipsis is the omission of a necessary word in a sentence because it is "understood," generally from previous text. A false ellipsis occurs when the necessary word is not clear or not to be found. Whereas false ellipsis errors may not be considered egregious, they are widespread.

False ellipsis: As the campaign progressed, I found him getting under my skin in a way that few people ever have.

The missing word, the word required to complete the sentence, may be "done," or "gotten," neither of which appears previously.

Better: As the campaign progressed, I found him getting under my skin in a way that few people ever have done.

Best: As the campaign progressed, I found him getting under my skin in a way that few *other* people ever have done.

There is also a logical error: "few other *people" is required because "him" is a person.*

Poor: He thinks he should be enjoying this experience more than he actually does.

Better: He thinks he should be enjoying this experience more than he actually does enjoy it.

Poor: I was feeling better than I had in years.

Better: I was feeling better than I had felt in years.

Correct: He wanted to do more than he was able.

This is grammatically correct because the elliptical words "to do" appear earlier in the expression.

Also correct: He wanted to do more than he was able to do.

Figurative Sense

Do not over-use words in a figurative sense if there are other words available which literally express your thought more accurately.

Poor: Gates singled out the use of pilot-less surveillance planes, in growing demand by commanders in Iraq and Afghanistan, as an example of how the Air force must act more aggressively.

Better: ...must act more energetically.

Better: ...must act more vigorously.

Better: ...must act more effectively.

Poor: The paint in this bucket is awesome.

Better: The paint in this bucket has a beautiful color.

Better: The paint in this bucket is very smooth.

Better: The paint in this bucket is water soluble, making it easy to clean the brushes.

Forbid -- Forbade

The past tense of forbid is forbade. It is pronounced "fore-bad" and rhymes with "glad."

Further -- Farther

Use "further" with degree.
Use "farther" with distance or measure.

Incorrect: Japan is *further* away than New York.

Correct: Japan is *farther* away than New York. (distance)

Correct: The *further* I proceed in my studies, the more interesting they get. (degree)

Best: The further I proceed in my studies, the more interesting they become. (Ruge disliked the excessive use of *get* and *got.*)

Incorrect: I have gone farther in my studies of German than I have in Spanish.

Correct: I have gone *further* in my studies of German than I have in Spanish. (in my studies of Spanish)

Gerunds -- Use of the Possessive with Gerunds

The subject of a gerund, if expressed, should be in the possessive case. (This traditional rule is often, if not usually, ignored by modern writers.)

Incorrect: Richard protested openly against his brother George being put to death.

Correct: Richard protested openly against his brother George's being put to death.

There is a certain logic here. He was not protesting against his brother George.

Also correct: Richard protested openly his brother George's being put to death.

Note: "Protest" can be a transitive verb, taking a direct object.

Incorrect: I hate him talking all the time.

Correct: I hate his talking all the time.

Note: It is not him *I hate, but* his *talking. (Also, in the sentence "I hate him talking," talking is not a gerund, but a participle -- an adjective.)*

But
Correct: I hate mosquitoes, always biting me when I go to the beach.

Note: It is not merely getting bitten at the beach that I hate, but the mosquitoes themselves that I hate.

Healthy -- Healthful

"Healthy" means IN good health; "healthful" means CONDUCIVE to good health.

Incorrect: In a nation with millions of overweight young people, the overall message to eat healthy is getting lost in a polarized meat-versus--vegetarian debate.

Correct: ...the overall message to eat *healthfully* is getting lost...

Furthermore: The doubly incorrect example here also gives an incorrect use of an adjective (healthy) where an adverb is called for.

Incorrect: The officers were on Capitol Hill advocating for passage of a nutrition bill that aims to make the nation's school lunches healthier.

Better: The officers were on Capitol Hill advocating for passage of a nutrition bill that aims to make the nation's school lunches *more healthful*.

Best -- Correct: The officers were on Capitol Hill advocating the passage of a nutrition bill that aims to make the nation's school lunches *more healthful*.

"Advocate" is a transitive verb. "Advocating something" is correct. "Advocating for something" is incorrect, substandard, or colloquial, although gaining in common usage. (See "Transitive Verb Requires Object." p 48.)

I -- Me

We all know that "I" is the nominative case form and "me" the objective case form. However, in some instances "me" is gradually replacing "I" and virtually becoming standard in English.

Common: Who's there? It's me.

Traditionally correct: It is I.

Correct: Johnny and I went to camp last summer.

Common but incorrect: Me and Johnny went to camp last summer.

Some English-speakers feel they should resist this trend and consequently may try too hard to speak correct English. We learn in the third grade that "I" is a good word and that "me" is a bad word. We are told, "Don't say, 'Me and Johnny,' say 'Johnny and I'." The problem is that we don't remember where that rule should be applied, so we sometimes make the choice that seems unnatural, hoping that it therefore will sound scholarly and erudite. Accordingly, many important people, sometimes even St. Albans graduates, make egregious errors of the "Between You and I" variety. Such errors become so common and pervasive that, to many people, they ultimately may "sound all right." Certain evolutionary changes in English are acceptable; others are not. To some extent the distinction may be a matter of taste and judgement.

INCORRECT: Quotations from famous people who should have known better:

> *We've had conversations between Frank and I.*
> *What are the differences between he and President Mubarak?*
> *It is an unfortunate personal issue that is between he and Jenny.*
> *That's what happened to Dick Gephart and I in Iowa.*
> *She held our family, my brother and I, together through tough times.*
> *He married Michele and I.*
> *Victory goes to he who endureth to the end.*

I trust he and his team a lot.
You are kind to let my wife and I be here today.
It was a difficult decision for she and her husband to leave Iran.
No one except he and Mr. Voyles knew about these secret little chats.
Look at the bright side -- she's bringing you and I (to the party).
They want Alex and I to go back and sign books.
There are a couple of swells between he and the hole.
Explain to we lazy people why this important.
In Ken Starr, Clinton has his best friend. He ought to send he and his family around the world, on a world cruise.
What struck my colleague and I was Saddam Hussein's determination to build the bomb.
If you cannot pay this fine within two weeks, you must come back and speak to Judge Carroll or I.
President Bush generously invited Michele and I to go meet with him on Monday.
Whom do men say that I am?

These examples suggest that, unfortunately, it is not always necessary to have a command of good grammar to achieve success and attain important positions these days. People who do have such command constitute an exclusive society in the United States -- join them and stay with them.

"If" Clauses – Subjunctive or Nominative?

Use the indicative if there is a possibility *of its being true.*
Use the subjunctive if there is no *possibility of its being true..*

Correct: If he *was* there, the bartender must have seen him. (He might have been there.)   Nominative

Correct: If he *were* there, the bartender would have seen him. (He wasn't there.) Subjunctive

Correct: If I *were* you, I would study a little more.   (I am not you.) Subjunctive

Correct: She said that if I was interested I could attend the elaborate ritual. (She believes I might be interested.)

Correct: She said that if I were interested I could have attended the elaborate ritual. (She knew I was not interested.)

Impact (verb) -- Affect

Do not use impact *as a verb to mean* affect.

Impact means to *jam together*, or *compress*, and its past participle, *impacted*, means *jammed together*, as in the expression *impacted teeth*.

Correct: I had to have my number-sixteen wisdom-tooth extracted because it was impacted.

Incorrect: Percival's lifestyle was *impacted* by his winning of the lottery.

Correct: Percival's lifestyle was *affected* by his winning of the lottery.

Incorrect: I fear the proposed tax law will *impact* our business.

Correct: I fear the proposed tax law will *affect* our business.

Poor: He is an impact football player.

Better: He is a *powerful* football player. (*adjective*)

Note: The use of impact *and various derivations therefrom has become pervasive in modern colloquial English. The student would do well to avoid using all these modern colloquial forms of* impact, *replacing them with standard words of clearer or more precise meaning.*

Impact (noun) – Effect

Impact *as a noun may mean* effect, *a noun.*

Correct: His winning of the lottery had quite an effect on Percival's lifestyle.

Correct: His winning of the lottery had quite an impact on Percival's lifestyle.

Correct: The impact of the crash could be felt a block away.

Correct: The impact of the meteorite left a crater a quarter of a mile wide.

Do not use impact *with other meanings than those given above.*

Incredible -- Unbelievable

Do not use incredible *or* unbelievable *to mean* remarkable, surprising, astonishing, *etc. Use the proper and most precise word to express your thought. Avoid the use of vague or meaningless words.*

Poor, meaningless: You should have seen the Dallas Cowboys Sunday; they were incredible.

Better: You should have seen the Dallas Cowboys Sunday;   they were terrible.

Better: You should have seen the Dallas Cowboys Sunday;   they were spectacular.

Poor: Our new drama teacher is unbelievable.

Better: Our new drama teacher is extremely ugly.

Better: Our new drama teacher is a terrible actor.

Better: Our new drama teacher is a superb actor.

Better: Our new drama teacher knows her Shakespeare backwards and forwards.

Incredulous -- Incredible

Incredulous *means* not believing *or* very skeptical. *It describes a person confronted with something that is* not to be believed *and which therefore is* incredible *in the proper sense of that word. (Unfortunately it has become popular to use* incredible, *and* unbelievable, *in some different sense, with little, or vague, meaning. -- See above, p 23.)*

Incorrect: The witness gave an incredulous story, and the jury did not believe it.

Correct: The witness gave an *incredible* story; the jury did not believe it.

Correct: The witness gave such a far-fetched story that the jury was incredulous.

Incredible *and* unbelievable *have been so frequently and so badly used that it may be better to avoid use of these words whenever possible.*

In Excess of – More than

Do not use the expression in excess of *to mean* more than *unless there is a good reason for doing so.*

Incorrect: The British lost *in excess of* 450 ships to privateers in 1777.

Correct: The British lost *more than* 450 ships to privateers in 1777.

Correct, but awkward: The British losses to privateers were in excess of 450 ships in 1777.

Correct, but poor: The British losses to privateers exceeded 450 ships in 1777.

Note: When one uses the expression "in excess of," or "exceeded," there is an implication that the number cited has a certain significance.

Correct: My expenditures on books last week *exceeded* my allowance.

Correct, but awkward: My expenditures on books last week were *in excess of* my allowance.

Correct: The weight of my baggage was in excess of sixty-six pounds (sixty-six pounds being the limit of free baggage allowed, hence a significant number).

Correct: The weight of my baggage exceeded sixty-six pounds.

Poor: The weight of my baggage was in excess of fifty pounds.

Better: My baggage weighed more than fifty pounds.

Note: Sixty-six pounds is the equivalent of thirty kilograms.

Avoid Lapses of Logic, and Stupidities

Make sure your sentence cannot be misread to imply something you did not intend. A sentence must make sense, not merely grammatically but also logically and sensibly.

These are actual examples of stupidities and lapses of logic taken from the media. Most of them came from important national figures. Some of them are humorous; all of them are lamentable.

I wouldn't be surprised if we didn't see action soon.

In August, 1942, when the Marines began the re-conquest of the Solomon Islands, they came ashore in waves.

The United States, for all its faults, is still the greatest nation in the country.

Tonight is definitely not his day.

Tune in tomorrow for the next episode of "How I Met Your Mother" followed by "The Big Bang Theory."

The Texas House endorsed death sentences for habitual child predators and harsher penalties for other offenders.

The Sumter Gallery of Art is a state-of-the-art facility.

We need more clean needles to penetrate the AIDS problem in the African-American community.

That outcrop, there in the distance, is just out of this world.
  (NASA scientist, viewing photograph taken by Mars Rover)

The breast cancer clinic on Hilton Head uses cutting-edge technology.

I would not be surprised if they didn't bring in a new quarterback.

The Circuit Court of Appeals held that the officers were justified in making an arrest because Brookes was resisting arrest.

If credit continues to dry up it will trickle down and affect small businesses.

The odds of making a royal flush are 649,740 to one.

Those at the top of the social ladder desire to maintain their wealth whatever the cost.

Dad's father died when he was five.

Here in the box we are very close in terms of proximity to the players.

I knew the odds of not having another casualty were not very low.

Small-town mayors have a tough job. That is where the rubber hits the road. They have to fill the pot holes and trim the trees.

We know for sure that Bin Laden is either in Afghanistan, or in another country, or dead.

Clinton's other core argument is that she is ready, tested, and strong while her opponent is unproven and thin-skinned.

Consumer spending was negative in June, after adjusting for inflation.

It's not a widespread event for any one particular location.

He flew out to centerfield.

The company expects lower than expected earnings.

He's been battling colon cancer head on.

An attack against a Mehsud compound killed more than two dozen militants, who quickly retrieved the remains of their fallen comrades.

They were under strict orders not to commit mayhem unless it was absolutely necessary to save lives.

What we're trying to do is to try and stay focused on what we're trying to do.

It's important that these essential things be continued.

He was charged in the murder of his late wife.

Fasten seat belt while seated.

Rives Allard's father had died when he was nine years old.

Greens Creek Mining Company has received numerous awards because of its cutting-edge environmental practices.

When he died he was one of the few high-ranking Confederate officers still alive.

In the two decades 1860 to 1880 the number of landholdings in Louisiana multiplied by 89 per cent.

Last year the lottery paid out an average of 3.2 billion dollars.

The buildings and stores of the city seemed old, as if built before the turn of the century or earlier.

I wouldn't be surprised if we didn't see a new pitcher.,

The gun had been stolen at some point since its manufacture.

Our troops have done a bang-up job.

As Scott had predicted, it proved less difficult than anticipated.

This is the best team record-wise in the National League.

It doesn't bother me to live next door to a black person or anybody else as long as they don't bother me.

There is snow-shower activity in the Chicago area at the present time.

The pastor is praying that the fire doesn't reach his church.

By then Tebaldi was dead, so they thought it would be better to get someone else.

Less -- Fewer

Use less *with nouns of measure and* fewer *with nouns of count.*

Correct: I have less land than he has. (*Land* is a noun of measure.)

Incorrect: I have less acres than he has.

Correct: I have fewer acres than he has. (*Acres* is a noun of count.)

Incorrect: There are less stars in the Southern Hemisphere than in the Northern Hemisphere.

Correct: There are *fewer* stars in the Southern Hemisphere than in the Northern Hemisphere.

Incorrect: My cousin has six less chickens than I have.

Correct: My cousin has six fewer chickens than I have.

Numbers usually introduce nouns of count.   But:

Incorrect: Annapolis is fewer than forty miles from Washington.

Correct: Annapolis is less than forty miles from Washington.

Less *is used with numbers when they are an expression of measurement.*

Correct: The town had a population of less than 3500.

Correct but less common: The town had a population of fewer than 3500.

NOTE: "Population" is an unusual noun in so far as in modern usage it has come to be considered either a noun of measure or a noun of count.

Also correct: The population of the town was under 3500.

(*See* UNDER -- LESS THAN, p 51)

"Let's" Means "Let us"

An appositive always agrees in case with the word with which it is in apposition.

Incorrect: Look, Mr. Grant, let's you and I start at the very beginning of this thing.

Here "you and I" should read "you and me" as it is in apposition with "us." ("let's" means "let us.")

Correct: Look, Mr. Grant, let's you and me start at the very beginning of this thing.

Incorrect: Let's you and I go away together.

This is a very common error. It is the equivalent of saying, "Let I go," or "Allow I to go."

Correct: Let's you and me go away together.

Note: The "us" of "let's" ("let us") is in the objective case as it is the subject of an infinitive. (go = to go).

LIE and LAY -- SIT and SET

Remember that lie *and* sit *are intransitive verbs whereas* lay *and* set *are transitive verbs (and take an object).*

Incorrect: Let sleeping dogs lay.

Correct: Let sleeping dogs lie.

Correct: Now I lay me down to sleep.

Correct: Just lay the books on the table, please.

Incorrect: She returned with the beer mugs and sat them on the table.

Correct: She returned with the beer mugs and set them on the table.

Incorrect: Did you sit the baby in the high chair?

Correct: Did you set the baby in the high chair?

Incorrect: My grandparents were just setting there on the porch.

Correct: My grandparents were just sitting there on the porch.

Dumbbell aid: Why was George Washington buried standing?

Correct: Because he couldn't lie.

Like

Do not use "like" in written or spoken English to mean "for instance,"
"well," "approximately," " ya know," "duh," or for no reason at all.

Incorrect: He was, like, walking down the street.

Correct: He was walking down the street.

Incorrect: They've only hit, like, 20 homers in this park all year.

Correct: They've hit only 20 homers in this park all year.

Correct: They've hit only about 20 homers in this park all year.

Like -- As If, As Though

Do not use the preposition "like" when a conjunction is called for to
introduce a clause. "As if" and "as though" are conjunctions.

Incorrect: It looks like it will rain.

Correct: It looks as though it will rain.

Correct: It looks like another rainy day.

Incorrect: He ran like his pants were on fire.

Correct: He ran as if his pants were on fire.

Myself -- Me -- I

Do not use "myself" when "me" (or "I") is called for.   Myself, himself,
themselves, *etc., are reflective or intensive forms only..*

Incorrect: My three platoon commanders and myself had a carriage to
ourselves.

Correct: My three platoon commanders and I had a carriage to ourselves.

Incorrect: They saw all three of us: Tom, Dick, and myself.

Correct: They saw all three of us: Tom, Dick, and me.

Correct: I cut myself trying to shave. (*reflexive*)

Correct: We had a carriage to ourselves. (reflexive)

Correct: I myself took full responsibility. (*intensive*)

Correct: The king himself spoke to the crowd. (*intensive*)

Correct: He pressed 250 pounds; I couldn't do that myself. (*intensive*)

*The rule also applies, of course, to "herself," "yourself," "themselves,"
etc.*

Not Help But

Although it is in common use by many esteemed writers, the expression "could not help but" *does not withstand rigorous grammatical analysis. The use of both* "help" *and* "but" *in this fashion in the same phrase is at least unnecessary and perhaps even redundant.*

Questionable: Edna could not help but think that she had been very careless.

Correct: Edna could not help think that she had been very careless.

Correct: Edna could not but think that she had been very careless.

Questionable: I could not help but take Mr. Keyes seriously.

Correct: I could not help take Mr. Keyes seriously.

Correct: I could not but take Mr. Keyes seriously.

Correct: I could not help taking Mr. Keyes seriously.

One of Those Who . . .

The expression "one of those who..." *calls for a plural verb.*

Incorrect: William Saffire is one of those men who always manages to wind up in the middle of things.

Correct: William Saffire is one of those men who always *manage* to wind up in the middle of things.

Here the subject of manage *is* who, *and the antecedent of* who *is* men, *not* William Saffire.

Incorrect: I am one of those who believes that it would be a mistake for the US to take unilateral action.

Correct: I am one of *those who believe* that it would be a mistake for the US to take unilateral action.

Better still: I am one of those who believe that it would be a mistake for the United States to take unilateral action.

Correct: I am *one who believes* that it would be a mistake for the United States to take unilateral action.

Incorrect: I am one of those people who has a step-mother and a step-father.

Correct: I am one of *those people who have* a step-mother and a step-father.

Correct: I am *one who has* a step-mother and a step-father.

Overworked Preposition

A single preposition does not suffice where two are required.

Incorrect: It was one of those subjects I depended on others for guidance.

"For" is an overworked preposition, with two objects, namely "which" (understood) and "guidance." At the very least, two "for's" are required.

Better: It was one of those subjects I depended on others for, for guidance.

Better yet: It was one of those subjects for which I depended on others for guidance.

Incorrect: The mate, as he was known in the days of sail, is the one who must ensure that things are shipshape.

"As" is overworked; another "as" is needed. Whereas it may sound repetitive to say it, it is correct to say, "The mate, as he was known as in the days of sail..." Or else the sentence could be rewritten.

Correct: The mate, as he was known *as* in the days of sail, is the one who must ensure that things are shipshape.

Correct, perhaps better: He was known as mate in the days of sail, and he is the one who must ensure that things are shipshape.

Incorrect: It is impossible to enjoy affluence with the felicity it is capable of being enjoyed, while so much misery is mingled in the scene.

Correct: It is impossible to enjoy affluence with the felicity *with which* it is capable of being enjoyed, while so much misery is mingled in the scene.

Participles Ending with -ing

Do not drop the "-ing" ending of a present participle without a good reason for doing so.

Poor: We estimate your wait time to be between two and four minutes.

Better: We estimate your *waiting* time to be between two and four minutes.

Poor: On Thursday, Feb 7, 2002 Bush reviewed the refined "Start Plan" for war with Iraq with Gen. Franks and his national security team.

Better: ...Starting Plan...

Poor: The Cowboys need to work on their run game.

Better: The Cowboys need to work on their *running* game.

Correct: My brother John is on the swimming team.

Common: My brother John is on the US Olympic Swim Team.

Poor: The trade post sat on a little level patch of ground.

Better: The *trading* post sat on a little level patch of ground.

Poor: Rob's Reliable Tow Service is open 24 hours a day.

Better: Rob's Reliable *Towing* Service is open 24 hours a day.

Poor: He was a star of the Columbia debate team.

Unfortunately, our tendency to drop the --ing ending of the present participle is strong and widespread, and seems likely to continue growing.

Past Perfect Tense -- Past Tense

Do not use the past perfect tense when the past tense is called for.
Ensure correct sequence of tenses.

Incorrect: Before Reeves killed himself he had tried repeatedly to convince his wife to commit suicide with him.

Correct: Before Reeves killed himself he tried repeatedly to convince his wife to commit suicide with him.

Correct: Reeves had tried repeatedly to convince his wife to commit suicide with him when he killed himself.

Incorrect: She looked up and down the street after she had passed through the gate.

Correct: She looked up and down the street after she passed through the gate.

Correct: She looked up and down the street when she had passed through the gate.

Correct: She looked up and down the street after passing through the gate.

Correct: Having passed through the gate, she looked up and down the street.

Incorrect: Rowan had adored his wife. While she was living he had led the life of an ordinary planter.

Correct: Rowan had adored his wife. While she was living he *led* the life of an ordinary planter.

Incorrect: When Isabel died he had been certain that she was poisoned.

Correct: When Isabel died he was certain she had been poisoned.

Plus – Furthermore

Avoid using plus *as a conjunction meaning* furthermore, moreover, *or* besides.

Colloquial: Carl was getting old; plus, Mrs. Osborne did not need his help anyway -- she was able to take care of herself.

Correct: Carl was getting old; *furthermore*, Mrs. Osborne did not need his help anyway -- she was able to take care of herself.

Correct: Carl was getting old; *moreover*, Mrs. Osborne did not need his help anyway -- she was able to take care of herself.

Colloquial: He is a committed man; plus he has an imagination.

Correct: He is a committed man; *besides,* he has an imagination.

Correct: He is a committed man; *furthermore,* he has an imagination.

Correct: I have two dogs plus a cat.

Better yet: I have two dogs and a cat.

Loss of Prepositions Associated with Verbs

Some verbs have a special meaning when associated with certain prepositions. This meaning may be lost or changed if the preposition is dropped.

Incorrect: It's a matter for the feds, and we'll tip them when the time is right. (one city policeman to another)

Correct: It's a matter for the feds, and we'll tip them *off* when the time is right.

There is a significant difference between "tipping them" and "tipping them off." A lot of meaning is being lost as such "verb-associated prepositions" are gradually and inexorably being dropped from the American English language.

Incorrect: The serial number (of the gun) had been filed.

Correct: The serial number of the gun had been filed *off.*

Incorrect: The temple of king Mausolus was a place to be taken after death.

Correct: The temple of king Mausolus was a place to be taken *to* after death.

Poor: US officials say the terrorists are seeking new places to operate, including Yemen.

Better: US officials say the terrorists are seeking new places to operate *in,* including Yemen.

Incorrect: The house was built in the late 1960's for the owner's mother-in-law to live.

Correct: The house was built in the late 1960's for the owner's mother-in-law to live *in.*

Poor: Police units were hunting Fidel Castro.

Better: Police units were hunting *for* Fidel Castro.

Correct: Police units were seeking Fidel Castro.

Hunt, *without the preposition, generally means to* pursue and kill *(game or prey)* for food or sport, *as* to hunt buffalo *or* bear.

Hunt for *means* to seek *or* to search for.

Poor: Our crisis is global, so there's no place to flee.

The expression (poor) to flee a place *(without a preposition) would mean* to leave a place.

Correct: Our crisis is global, so there's no place *to which* to flee.

Becoming acceptable: Our crisis is global, so there's no place to flee *to.*

Note: Ruge did not like terminal prepositions if they could be avoided without awkwardness. Churchill is reputed to have said, "This silly rule is something up with which I will not put." Ruge summed the matter up, saying, "A preposition is a bad thing to end a sentence with."

Poor: My wife's car was towed because she parked by a fire hydrant.

Correct: My wife's car was towed *away* because she parked by a fire hydrant.

Sometimes the associated word may be an adverb (away). Towed away *has a different meaning than* towed.

Correct: My wife towed our trailer from Silver Spring to Southwest Harbor.

Someplace -- Some Place

These terms are not synonymous. Someplace *is an adverb:* some *(as used here) is an adjective, and* place *is a noun.*

Incorrect: Generally, when they took off for the evening, they had a specific place to go.

Correct: Generally, when they took off for the evening, they had a specific place to go *to.*

Whereas it is possible "to go someplace," it is not possible "to go a place." The same holds for somewhere, anywhere, anyplace, *etc.*

Incorrect: Generally, in the evening, they liked to go some place together.

Correct: Generally, in the evening, they like to go someplace together.

Correct: Generally, in the evening, they liked to go *to* some place together. (perhaps a quiet place)

Incorrect: They spent the weekend some place on Lake Como.

Incorrect: They spent the weekend on Lake Como some place.

Correct: They spent the weekend someplace on Lake Como.

Correct: They spent the weekend on lake Como someplace.

Here "someplace" is an adverb modifying "spent." "On Lake Como" is an adverbial phrase also modifying "spent." (They spent the weekend someplace, and *they spent the weekend on Lake Como.)*

Correct: They spent the weekend *at* some place on Lake Como.

Here "on Lake Como" *is an adjective phrase modifying "place."*

Incorrect: South Carolina is now known in Hollywood as a great state to make films.

Correct: South Carolina is now known in Hollywood as a great state to make films *in*.

Correct: South Carolina is now known in Hollywood as a great state *in which* to make films.

Incorrect: As a Secret Service agent she'd never gone anywhere without her gun, not even the toilet. *(One doesn't "go the toilet.")*

Correct: As a Secret Service agent she'd never gone anywhere without her gun, not even *to* the toilet.

Incorrect: It would be a beautiful place to live, and I liked the people immediately. *(One doesn't "live a place.")*

Correct: It would be a beautiful place to live *in*, and I liked the people immediately.

Special Plurals

Some words of foreign origin have unusual plural forms in English that can be matters of disagreement and debate. One should remember that we are now speaking and writing English, not Latin or Italian or some other language.

Questionable: Where are the data on last year's corn production in Iowa?

Correct: Where is the data on last year's corn production in Iowa?

Although in Latin data *is the plural of* datum, *in many of its uses in English* data *is properly treated as a singular noun (like* news, *which, interestingly enough, is expressed by a plural noun in many foreign languages).*

Correct: Many specific data on corn production were collected from 947 Iowa farmers over a six-month period.

In this case data *is viewed as "pieces of information." A piece of information, or* datum, *is of course the singular of* data.

Correct: The spaghetti is very good tonight.

Questionable: The spaghetti are very good tonight.

Spaghetti *has become a singular word in English, although it is still plural in Italian. (Gli spaghetti sono buoni stasera.)*

Questionable: I dropped a spaghetto on the floor.

Correct: I dropped a piece of spaghetti on the floor.

Note: The point here is that we are now speaking English and applying English grammar to English words of foreign origin.

Correct: We have a long agenda today.

In English agenda *means a list of items to be considered, although, being the plural form in Latin, it apparently once meant the* items *on such a list, each of which was an* agendum.

Correct: The actors were wearing togas. (*not* togae, *unless you are are trying frightfully hard to sound erudite*)

Correct (advertisement): Shop a quality collection of candelabras at Hayneedle.

Candelabra *has become an acceptable singular form in standard English, and* candelabras *an acceptable plural form, although we still hear the affected sounding* candelabrum *occasionally.*

Correct: The news media is a powerful force in the United States.

Correct: The media have no taste and are always looking for scandal.

Note: Media, *as in* news media, *may take either a singular or plural verb.* Medium, *the Latin singular of* media, *is not often used in this sense in English.*

Subjunctive Falling into Disuse

The use of the subjunctive is gradually fading from the English language, but certain standards remain.

Unacceptable: All this might have been nothing if Wang Lung were still a poor man or if the water was not spread on his fields.

This strange example of the decaying use of the subjunctive contains two spots in which the subjunctive is called for, but employed in only one of them. Traditional grammar calls for "if Wang Lung were still" and "if the water were not spread." The modern trend away from the subjunctive would have "was" in each case. Whereas I still prefer the subjunctive in cases "contrary to fact," consistency is necessary in any case.

Somewhat better: All this might have been nothing if Wang Lung was still a poor man or if the water was not spread on his fields.

Best -- Correct: All this might have been nothing if Wang Lung were still a poor man or if the water *were* not spread on his fields.

Incorrect (but gaining in popularity): Eggworthy hurtled through the air as though a giant metal device was intent on scrambling him.

Correct: Eggworthy hurtled through the air as though a giant metal device *were* intent on scrambling him.

Incorrect (but gaining in popularity): I want you to imagine that Hillary Clinton was President of the United States.

Correct: I want you to imagine that Hillary Clinton *were* President of the United States.

Incorrect: If he would have been taught younger, he would have been a great champion.

Correct: If he had been taught younger, he would have been (or *would be*) a great champion.

The incorrect, but common, use of the conditional form of a verb when the subjunctive is called for is discussed herein under the heading WOULD -- WOULD, p 59.

That for Very

Do not use that *when* very *is called for.*

Incorrect: I did not sleep that well last night.

Correct: I did not sleep *very* well last night.

Correct: I did not know your little brother was that old.
(having just learned he was twelve years old)

Incorrect: I saw *Moon over Burma* on TV last night, and to tell the truth I didn't think it was that good.

Correct: I saw *Moon over Burma* on TV last night, and to tell the truth I didn't think it was very good.

Transitive Verb Requires Object

Incorrect or colloquial: All of them – Bishop Tutu, the Pope, President Carter – have advocated for clemency.

Correct: All of them – Bishop Tutu, the Pope, President Carter – have advocated clemency.

Incorrect or colloquial: He advocates for lifting the ban on "Don't Ask, Don't Tell."

Correct: He advocates lifting the ban on "Don't Ask, Don't Tell."

Incorrect or colloquial: The public policy group advocated against abortion and in support of traditional marriage.

Correct: The public policy group opposed abortion and advocated traditional marriage.

"Advocate" is a transitive verb. One advocates something. One does not advocate "for" something or "in support of" something.

Incorrect: She had grown up just north of the neighborhoods where I had organized.

Correct: She had grown up just north of the neighborhoods where I had organized the voters (or populace, or unions, or whatever).

"Organize" is a transitive verb and takes an object; one organizes something.

Two Subordinate Clauses

I am left unsatisfied by a sentence consisting of two subordinate clauses, although this subject has been discussed but little by most grammarians.

Questionable: Even though these horrors are not physically present, yet the conscience-ridden mind torments itself with its own goads and whips.

Better: Even though these horrors are not physically present, the conscience-ridden mind torments itself with its own goads and whips.

Also better: These horrors are not physically present, yet the conscience-ridden mind torments itself with its own goads and whips.

Questionable: Although we were outnumbered two to one, nevertheless our forces fought valiantly and were able to stem the enemy advance.

Better: Although we were outnumbered two to one, our forces fought valiantly and were able to stem the enemy advance.

Also better: We were outnumbered two to one;   nevertheless our forces fought valiantly and were able to stem the enemy advance.

Uncountable Nouns

Some nouns refer to things that cannot be counted..

Incorrect: This is one more evidence that the bright young men of the GOP are disappointing us.

Correct: This is one more *piece of* evidence that the bright young men of the GOP are disappointing us.

Evidence *is an uncountable noun.   We must say "piece of evidence," or "some evidence," or words to that effect.   Other such nouns may include* information, satisfaction, dismay, wisdom, knowledge, assistance, fortitude, courage, rectitude. *These words are used only in the singular and without the indefinite article "a" or "an."   One does not say "informations" in English, or "an information," although he may do the equivalent in French or some other foreign languages.*

Under -- Less Than

*There is a slight difference in the meanings of "under" and "less than"
which seems to be gradually disappearing. Traditionally, "less than"
generally refers to numbers and quantities, whereas "under" is more
likely to refer to conceptual amounts and spatial relationships. However
a more significant difference is sometimes one of grammatical form:*

Incorrect: He ran the mile in under four minutes.

Correct: He ran the mile in less than four minutes.

Correct: The winning time was under four minutes.

Correct: The winning time was less than four minutes.

*The problem here is that "in" is a preposition and requires a noun -- or a
group of words serving as a noun -- as its object.   On the one hand,
"under four minutes" is not a noun but a prepositional phrase modifying
"ran."   On the other hand, "less" is an adjective and "less than four
minutes" serves as a noun, namely "four minutes" with its adjective
modifier "less than."*

Incorrect: He ran up three flights of stairs with a bicycle and took the
garbage out in under two minutes.

Correct: He ran up three flights of stairs with a bicycle and took the
garbage out in *less than* two minutes.

Incorrect: The town had a population of under 3500.

Better: The population of the town was under 3500.

Correct: The town had a population under 3500.

*A prepositional phrase (*under 3500 *or* under four minutes*) may function as an adjective or adverb, but not as a noun. The object of a preposition, such as* of *or* in, *must be a noun.*

Correct: The town had a population of less than 3500.

Correct: The town had a population of fewer than 3500.

"Population" is an unusual noun in so far as in modern usage it can be considered either a noun of measure or a noun of count.
(See LESS -- FEWER, p 26.)

Incorrect: Get high-speed internet for as low as $39.95.

Correct: Get high-speed internet for as little as $39.95.

Also correct: Get high-speed internet for a price as low as $39.95.

"Low" is an adjective; the object of a preposition (for) must be a noun.

Note: Similar observations hold for OVER and MORE THAN.

Verb or Noun? -- Pronunciation

Some two-syllable words are verbs when the second syllable is stressed, but are nouns, or sometimes adjectives, when the first syllable is stressed.

Examples.

combat
conduct
conflict
detail
object
perfect
permit
rebel
recall
recess
reject
relay
replay
research
subject
suspect

Incorrect: I will give you the de<u>tails</u> later.

Correct: I will give you the <u>de</u>tails later.

Correct: I received a de<u>tailed</u> report on the matter.

Incorrect: The information was <u>re</u>layed to headquarters.

Correct: The information was re<u>layed</u> to headquarters.

Correct: Our track team won the <u>re</u>lay.

Correct: We won the <u>re</u>lay race.

Correct: I sus<u>pect</u> that the <u>sus</u>pect is guilty.

Warmer Temperatures -- Higher Temperatures

Temperature is properly described as being higher *or* lower.   *The weather, the day, the air, or an object may be* warmer *or* colder.

Incorrect: The temperature today is ten degrees hotter than it was yesterday.

Correct: The temperature today is ten degrees *higher* than it was yesterday.

Correct: Today New York is hotter than Atlanta.

Correct: The temperature in New York is higher than it is in Atlanta.

Correct: My new girlfriend is colder than my old one was.

Questionable: Cryogenics involves the study of extremely cold temperatures.

Correct: Cryogenics involves the study of extremely low temperatures.

Correct: Cryogenics involves the study of extremely cold conditions.

Which -- That

The distinction between the two is sometimes blurry, but normally "which" is the more specific, and "that" is the more general. "Which" is more likely to introduce non-restrictive material, whereas "that" is the better choice to introduce restrictive material.

Incorrect: Education is the most powerful weapon which you can use to change the world.

Correct: Education is the most powerful weapon *that* you can use to change the world. (restrictive)

Better yet: Education is the most powerful weapon that one can use to change the world. (Ruge preferred the use of *one* rather than *you*.)

Correct: Education is a powerful weapon, *which* you can use to change the world. (non-restrictive)

Note: Which *is preceded by a comma when followed by lengthy non-restrictive material.*

Incorrect: It is the spirit within which counts.

Correct: It is the spirit within *that* counts.

Correct: Nelson Mandela was blessed with an indomitable spirit, which never left him.

Incorrect: I have a copy of the last photograph of Lincoln that was taken in 1865 just before he died.

This is an example of the less common, but incorrect, use of that *when* which *is called for. As written here it implies that there were other photographs of Lincoln taken later, after 1865, i.e. after he died. Use* which *if the material being introduced is non-restrictive.*

Correct: I have a copy of the last photograph of Lincoln, *which* was taken in 1865 just before he died.

Correct: I have a copy of the last photograph of Lincoln, which was taken in 1865, just before he died. (Because Lincoln died early in 1865 the comma preceding "just" is optional.)

Who and Whom

Do not use whom *when* who *is called for.*

Incorrect: Whom do men say that I am?
            (Mark 9-27, King James Bible.)

Correct: *Who* do men say that I am?

Incorrect: I'm very disappointed in the actions of whomever did this.

Correct: I'm very disappointed in the actions of *whoever* did this.

Incorrect: She set up meetings with whomever would listen.

Correct: She set up meetings with *whoever* would listen.

Incorrect: Lord Dunsany fought for whomever happened to be king.

Correct: Lord Dunsany fought for whoever happened to be king.

Incorrect: Abbas was aging, and we couldn't take it for granted that his successor, whomever it would be, would be committed to peace.

Correct: Abbas was aging, and we couldn't take it for granted that his successor, *whoever* it would be, would be committed to peace.

Incorrect: Could I forgive everybody whom I believed had wronged me?

Correct: Could I forgive everybody *who* I believed had wronged me?

When "who" (or "whoever") is the subject of a subordinate clause, it is in the nominative case.   The   fact that it is may be preceded by a preposition or transitive verb sometimes misleadingly suggests that it should be in the objective case. This is a very common error. The entire subordinate clause may be the object of a verb or preposition.

Note: The trend in English is away from whom, *which in time may fall entirely from common use. However, there seem to be some people who think* whom *sounds erudite and use it even when it is not called for.*

Standard: Who are you looking for?

Traditionally correct: Whom are you looking for?

Correct and artificial: For whom are you looking?

Correct and artificial: Whom seeketh thou?

Standard: Who did you see there?

Correct and stuffy: Whom did you see there?

Incorrect: Just give the book to whomever asks for it.

Correct: Just give the book to *whoever* asks for it.

With Regard to -- Regards

If the intended meaning is "regarding," or "concerning," "with regard to" is preferable to "with regards to."

Poor: The Senate will get a vote with regards *to* Iraq.

Better: The Senate will get a vote with regard to Iraq.

Better still: The Senate will get a vote regarding Iraq.

Correct: In compliance with your request, I sent some flowers with your regards to his widow.

Correct: Give my regards to Broadway.

Incorrect: He drove through the intersection without regards for the red light.

Correct: He drove through the intersection without *regard* for the red light.

Correct: With regard to your latest offer, I regret to inform you that we cannot accept such severe conditions.

- Regards,

James P. Morrison,
Vice President
PDQ Corporation

Would -- Would

Do not use "would" in a hypothetical clause.
A hypothetical clause should be in the subjunctive mode.

Incorrect: If it would rain, my crops would benefit.

Correct: If it *were to* rain, my crops would benefit.

Correct: If it *rained,* my crops would benefit.

When a hypothetical clause (the if *clause) and a resultant clause are used together in a sentence, the hypothetical clause is in the subjunctive mode and the resultant clause (with* would*) is in the conditional.*

Incorrect: If that would have happened earlier, we would have won.

Correct: If that had happened earlier, we would have won.

"Would" is correctly used in a subjunctive clause or sentence expressing a wish:

Correct: I wish that it *would* rain.

Correct: Oh, if only she *would* be quiet!

Correct but archaic: Oh, *would* that it had happened earlier!